Mars Colonization
The Red Planet's Uncertain Future

Table of Contents

Chapter 1. Introduction

Amidst the fiery allure of a Martian sunset, curiosity blooms for what the future holds for the Red Planet. In this special report on Mars Colonization: The Red Planet's Uncertain Future, we journey into what stands between humanity and its next giant leap. Unearthing the mechanics of transforming a scientific theory into reality, this report elucidates complexities at a level everyone can appreciate. The obstacles faced in this stunning endeavor - from technological puzzles to logistical mazes, survival strategies to sociopolitical challenges - are peeled back layer by layer, intriguing any reader daring to dream about humanity's next cosmic address. Regardless if you're a steadfast astronaut or a casual stargazer, prepare to be captivated by the thrill, the beauty, and the sheer audacity of the mission at hand. Don't miss this opportunity to own your piece of the cosmos! Get your copy of the report today and journey into the Martian mystery with us.

Chapter 2. Colonizing Mars: The Dream

An ethereal dream visualized by many, holding a charm that transcends political boundaries and cultures, the colonization of Mars is a beacon of hope for humanity's future in space. This pursuit is not merely a quest for survival or an exercise in scientific exploration, but it's the testament to our insatiable curiosity and our yearning for discovery, adventure, and understanding the unknown.

2.1. The Allure of the Red Planet

Mars, our celestial neighbor, is often referred to as the Earth's 'twin.' Numerous similarities exist between the two planets, rendering Mars as a prime candidate for potential colonization. From its day length of roughly 24.6 hours, almost similar to Earth, to a wealth of minerals and the possibility of water, its appeal is irresistible. And, although the Martian surface is barren, harsh, and evidently inhospitable, it offers valuable resources that are both rare on Earth and essential for human life and technological advancement.

2.2. Strategic Requirements for Mars Colonization

Mars colonization could not occur without solving significant logistical puzzles and overcoming astronomical technological hurdles. The first and foremost of these is getting to Mars. Manned missions to Mars necessitate spacecraft development that is not solely reliable but also efficient, economical, and sustainably powered. Present models propose the use of the classic 'Hohmann Transfer Orbit' trajectory, which offers the shortest path to Mars, conserving energy. Extended travel durations, typically between 6-9 months, also invoke concerns for crew wellbeing, both psychologically and physically.

Long-term human survival on Mars necessitates sophisticated life-supporting technology. Current research is primarily focused on Mars-based habitats, usually involving a combination of locally sourced building materials and prefabricated modules sent from Earth. Yet another challenge is ensuring these habitats can shield colonists from harmful radiation and extreme temperatures while also recycling waste and air.

Moreover, there's a need for technology to exploit Mars' resources. From extracting water from the planet's icy poles to harnessing its plentiful CO_2 for fuel and oxygen production, these self-sustainability strategies are indispensable for a successful colonization.

2.3. Sociopolitical Aspects of Colonizing Mars

Colonization of Mars, or any celestial body for that matter, raises numerous sociopolitical questions and challenges. Recent space exploration has been largely a collection of individual and private enterprises rather than a globally coordinated effort. Accordingly, the need for exhaustive international space laws and regulations is imperative, emphasizing ethical considerations and the fair distribution of space-related benefits.

The social dynamics of a Mars colony would represent a unique facet of human experience. The planning and architectural design of the habitats, routines and roles involved in maintaining sustainable living, and the cultural and community aspects would combine to form a social ecology unlike any seen on Earth. Psychologically, prospective colonists face isolation, monotony, and the ever-present risk of catastrophe. It becomes an essential requirement to develop effective strategies for promoting mental well-being.

2.4. Economic Perspectives

Economic aspects play a pivotal role in the Mars colonization. Given the considerable investment required to establish a colony and sustain it, plans for recuperating costs are on the table. Mars's mineral wealth, especially in precious metals like platinum, make it an enticing prospect for mining. In addition, space tourism and scientific discovery programs offer potential recouping avenues. Nonetheless, the long-term financial model for Mars colonization remains in its embryonic stage, inviting economic debates and fostering innovative ideas to render this dream financially viable.

In this ambitious quest, appreciating the full panorama of Mars colonization entails acknowledging its monumental challenges because, for every ingenious solution we devise, new issues invariably arise, requiring our perennial adaptation. Yet, what truly titillates our collective fascination is the audacious hope that, despite these obstacles, we will succeed. The motivation lies not in the destination but the journey, culminating in the crystallization of our collective knowledge, effort, technology, and spirit into the foundation of a thriving Martian colony.

The colonization of Mars, despite its uncertainty, is a journey into the future, a testament to human resilience and innovation, and represents not just a coming-of-age tale for humanity, but a compelling vision of a future where we spread across the cosmos, expanding not only our survival chances but our psychological and cultural horizons, spreading the seeds of life and consciousness through the Universe.

Chapter 3. Unveiling The Red Planet: Geology and Climate

Reaching out to the stars has always been a part of human nature. Mars, our planetary neighbor, has long been that shining beacon in the night sky, igniting curiosity and wonder. As we set our sights on becoming interplanetary species, gaining a deep understanding of the Martian geology and climate sits at the forefront of this colossal endeavor.

3.1. The Drawing Board: Our Current Understanding of Martian Geology

As Earth-bound observers, our earliest understandings of Mars were primitive at best. But, with the advent of space technology, missions like Mariner, Viking, Mars Global Surveyor, and Mars Reconnaissance Orbiter, have afforded us astonishing insights into the Martian surface and beyond.

Peering through the lens of these missions, we see that Mars is a rocky planet, its surface replete with impact basins and volcanic landforms, much like our own Earth. Yet, striking distinctions persist. The Red Planet presents the highest known volcano and deepest, longest canyon in the solar system. Olympus Mons, the giant shield volcano, stands nearly 22 kilometers high, and the grand Valles Marineris stretches over 4000 kilometers long, reaching depths of nearly seven kilometers.

Taking center stage are the Northern Lowlands and the Southern Highlands, a dichotomy that contributes to the Martian topographical diversity. The Highlands, deeply cratered and reminiscent of the highland on Earth's moon, raise more questions than they answer. The Lowlands, meanwhile, hint towards possible plate tectonic activity in Mars's bygone era.

The trail of Martian geology leads us through a labyrinth of elemental composition. Iron oxide or 'rust,' gives the Martian surface its iconic tinge, leading to the sobriquet 'Red Planet.' This elemental palette comes enriched by silicon, oxygen, and other minerals, including significant deposits of olivine, pyroxene, and feldspar, much like the terrestrial basalt rock.

From a distance, Mars appears desiccated - a barren, dusty desert. However, extensive evidence reveals an unanticipated storyline - the history of water on Mars. Dry riverbeds, ancient flood plains, and polar ice caps bear testament to what might have been a water-laden past. The discovery of hydrated salts and underground ice lakes compels us to revisit our theories of Martian habitability.

3.2. Reading the Winds: The Martian Climate

Understanding Martian climate is instrumental not only for deciphering the planet's past, but also for planning a human future there. Mars has a thin atmosphere, composed primarily of carbon dioxide, with traces of nitrogen and argon. This thin atmosphere, combined with the planet's distance from the sun, results in a harsh climate, with mean temperatures lingering around -80 degrees Fahrenheit.

The Martian year, spanning about 687 Earth days, holds seasons akin to Earth, owing to Mars's similar axial tilt. Yet, the longer orbit translates to prolonged seasons, with southern winters being particularly severe due to the elliptical nature of Mars's orbit. During these frigid months, temperatures in the southern polar regions can plummet to less than -200 degrees Fahrenheit.

While Earthly images of a breezy day might render the concept of Martian wind banal, the reality stands starkly different. Enigmatic dust storms, a well-established part of the Martian climate system, can last for months and cover the entire planet. These storms influence temperature distribution and drive water vapor and dust around the planet, efficiently reshaping the Martian surface.

Furthermore, Martian climate traces reveal fluctuations in axial tilt, or 'obliquity,' impacting atmospheric density and leading to potentially drastic climate evolution. Over the past few million years, Mars has experienced ice ages, much similar to Earth, linked to these obliquity variations.

3.3. Piece of the Puzzle: Recurring Slope Lineae

Recurring Slope Lineae (RSL) are dark streaks that advance downslope during warm seasons, fade in colder seasons, and reappear annually. First identified by the Mars Reconnaissance Orbiter in 2011, RSLs sparked a debate about the possibility of transient liquid water on modern Mars. Later studies propose deliquescence, a process where certain salts can absorb water vapor from the atmosphere and liquefy, as a potential explanation. However, the exact mechanisms and implications regarding habitability remain elusive, ensuring that RSLs hold a critical spot in our Martian investigations.

3.4. Aiding the Astronauts: Weather Predictions

Robust forecasting models and weather prediction strategies are pivotal to any successful Mars mission. Spacecraft landing relies heavily on atmospheric conditions, and Martian weather could impact the efficiency of technologies like dust-covered solar panels. Understanding patterns of dust storm formation and the influence of atmospheric opacity on surface radiation might well be a lynchpin for humans surviving and thriving on Mars.

Unveiling the Red Planet offers us perspective - a glimpse into the cosmic clockwork, where celestial bodies harmonize in an age-old dance. Departing from our Earthly cradle, we journey to Mars carrying dreams of tomorrow, ready to carve our stories into the chronicles of cosmic history. The Martian geology and climate hold not just the secrets of this alien world, but possibly the future of human exploration and colonization.

Chapter 4. Technical Triumphs and Tribulations

As humankind prepares to take its next giant leap, venturing into the vast expanse of Mars, technology remains the critical lynchpin. It is the core enabler that opens the door civilization's new cosmic abode, while simultaneously presenting a host of tribulations that must be navigated with precision, ingenuity, and foresight.

4.1. Mars Rovers: Our Robotic Precursors

The robotic explorers - Mars rovers such as Pathfinder, Spirit and Opportunity, Curiosity, and Perseverance - are the unsung heroes of our Martian endeavors. Each represents a technological triumph, successfully traveling millions of miles through space to arrive at and explore our neighbouring Red Planet.

Pathfinder, the first wheeled vehicle to touch Martian soil back in 1997, signaled humanity's resounding success in landing a semi-autonomous machine on a foreign planet. Building on this triumph, Spirit, Opportunity, and Curiosity developed the framework of our understanding of Mars today, with discoveries indicating evidence of past water activity, diverse mineralogy, and potential habitability in the planet's history.

Perseverance, the latest rover, has an even more ambitious mission. Equipped with the most advanced suite of scientific instruments for astrobiological investigations, it aims to collect samples of Martian rock and soil, potentially setting the stage for future human missions.

Underpinning these feats are technological advancements spanning across areas such as propulsion, deep space communication, autonomous navigation and more. Nevertheless, each rover mission and every innovation highlights a range of tribulations - the difficulty of achieving precise landing, potential malfunction of rovers, limitations in power generation, just to name a few.

4.2. Orchestration of Precise Landing

Getting an object from Earth to Mars is an incredible feat in itself. However, landing it onto the Martian surface precisely and without incident magnifies the challenge exponentially. The Perseverance mission, for example, relied on a complex series of manoeuvres, dubbed "seven minutes of terror," that perfectly orchestrated heat shield deployment, parachute ejection, radar tracking, sky crane maneuvers and other intricate tasks - all autonomously and with a delayed signal to Earth.

Moreover, Mars' thin atmosphere, just 1% the density of Earth's, means it provides significantly less cushioning for descending spacecraft - making the landing process even more harrowing. Given these challenges, our capacity to land rovers accurately on Mars represents an astounding technological success.

4.3. Rover Resilience on Martian Terrain

The Martian landscape is not kind to its visitors. With rugged terrains, large temperature swings, and omnipresent dust storms, Mars is a relentless proving ground for the technical prowess and resilience built into these rovers.

Spirit and Opportunity were designed for a mission life of merely 90 Mars days, or sols. The fact that they continued to function for years (six years for Spirit and a whopping fourteen years for Opportunity) before finally succumbing to the planet's harsh conditions stands as a testament to the robustness of technology and the meticulousness of rover design and operations.

4.4. Power Generation: A Perennial Challenge

One of the most defining tribulations for Mars exploration is power generation. Solar panels, which powered earlier rovers, are subject to dust accumulation and fluctuations in sunlight availability due to Mars' inclination and dust storms. This led to the incorporation of radioisotope thermoelectric generators (RTGs) in Curiosity and Perseverance, which convert heat from the natural decay of radioactive elements into electric power.

Still, power remains a critical constraint for rover operations and significantly more so for human missions, which will necessitate reliable power sources for maintaining life support systems, power habitats, drive construction and mining equipment, and more.

4.5. Towards a Sustainable Mars Colony

As we envision a human outpost on Mars, the required technology scales in complexity manifold. The sustainability of life in a long-term Mars colony necessitates technological advances in areas such as life support systems, in-situ resource utilization (ISRU, essentially living off the land), and the development of radiation-shielding habitats, among others.

However, the trial and tribulation-filled saga of technological evolution carries the promise of triumph as well. As we continue to surmount these challenges, the picture of a prosperous human existence on Mars will become less of a dream and more of a tangible, reachable reality. To construct such a reality, what we need is perseverance to contest every tribulation and the spirit to celebrate every triumph along the way. And if history is any indication, it is this very battle that humankind excels in. The Red Planet awaits.

Chapter 5. Logistical Leaps: Preparing for the Interplanetary Journey

Logistical planning for an interplanetary mission is a multifaceted task, where every item counts, and every pound of payload must be optimized. Grounding our understanding in the present state of space missions and drawing from humanity's history of voyaging the unknown, our jump off point includes everything from essential mission planning maneuvers to the fascinating conundrums of food, fuel, equipment, and human needs.

5.1. Planning The Martian Voyage

Years before the mission can commence, the planning phase painstakingly decides every crucial aspect of the journey. It's not just about 'getting there.' It is the harmony of scheduling to align with the Mars window, precision in course plotting to save energy, and astute anticipation of spacecraft health and maintenance needs.

Every 26 months, a unique opportunity - called a Mars launch window - opens, when the alignment of Earth and Mars is just right for a mission. This timeframe is critical to conserve precious fuel and resources during transit. However, the window doesn't bid us time luxury. A delay in launch could result in prolonging the mission until the next window, instigating massive cost overruns and logistical headaches.

The interplanetary journey from Earth is estimated to be roughly six to nine months long, with a distance of about 225 million kilometers. It is essential to calculate the spacecraft's trajectory accurately, often using a method called 'Hohmann transfer orbit,' to minimize fuel usage. This involves a 'free return' trajectory, where the spacecraft swings around Mars and comes back to Earth in the event of a failed system. Planning also caters for onboard breakdown possibilities, requiring redundancy of critical parts and preplanned failure response systems.

5.2. The Puzzle of the Payload

Let's delve into the specifics of the spacecraft payload. A delicate course lies between packing sufficient resources for survival and safeguarding the mission's economic viability. The cost of carrying each additional kilogram to Mars is stupefying.

The main aspects of the payload puzzle can be broadly categorized into human resources, equipment, and propellant. The human resources for a Mars mission include water, food, and oxygen. NASA's Mars Design Reference Architecture proposes having enough supplies for about 500 days for a crew of six. Food and water can be recycled to a certain extent, but a ready supply must exist for emergencies.

Equipment onboard the spacecraft must be multi-purpose and modular in design, aimed at working in harmony with the physical and psychological needs of the crew. It must commit space efficiency for habitation, research, system maintenance, and entertainment.

A stunning proportion of the payload is propellant. Current chemical rockets will necessitate multiple launches for refueling in Earth's orbit, adding complexity and cost. However, the evolution of nuclear and electric propulsion technologies may alleviate this astonishing need for fuel, reducing overall project costs and logistics.

5.3. Preparing Astronauts: Human Factors

The interplanetary expedition also incites a blend of biological and psychological challenges. A prolonged journey in a cramped spacecraft, amidst an expanse of stark emptiness, can inherently lead to potentially disastrous psychological breakdowns. Rigorous psychological screening is warranted, and onboard mental health resources should be a critical component of the payload.

On the other hand, the physical health of astronauts is a key determinant in mission success. The hazards of a low-gravity environment, such as muscle and bone loss, vision degradation, and radiation exposure, require preemptive countermeasures and onboard biological maintenance.

The importance of packing skills and expertise within the mission crew can't be overstated. Contrary to popular belief, astronauts aren't just brilliant scientists. They are engineers, doctors, physicists, pilots, mechanics, and much more. The mission demands a functional mélange of robust expertise to navigate unanticipated obstacles.

5.4. Logistics of Return

A topic frequently debated is whether the manned Mars mission should be one-way or roundtrip. The logistics of return dramatically increase the mission's complexity and risk. Yet, the compelling moral argument remains, of not abandoning pioneers on a far-off world.

Staging a return voyage demands more fuel, additional spacecraft, and specialized equipment. Pondering upon the idea of 'live off the land,' fuel required for the trip back could be theoretically manufactured on Mars itself, via the In-Situ Resource Utilization (ISRU) strategy. Yet, the practicality of that notion is currently bridled by technological hurdles.

In summary, the logistical design of venturing to Mars is an intricate balance, brimming with economic, technological, and human factors. From planning launch windows to managing psychological health, this pursuit calls upon the best of humanity's innovative and collaborative abilities. While immense challenges lie ahead, meticulous planning paired with cutting-edge technology, may make the dream of colonizing the Red Planet, a tangible reality. It's truly the sci-fi of the present era: our potential destiny, etched into the Martian soil, awaits our arrival, biding its time under the Martian sunsets.

Chapter 6. Surviving Mars: Essential Resources and Habitability

Establishing a successful Mars colony will require the identification, extraction, and utilization of essential resources for survival on the Martian surface. Among these imperative resources are water, a breathable atmosphere, shelter, food, and energy sources that can withstand Mars's inhospitable conditions. To truly understand the complexity of this endeavor, we must delve into the reality of acquiring and maintaining these resources.

6.1. Water: The Elixir of Life

Water is fundamental to life as we understand it. On Mars, water exists, but not as we often encounter it on Earth. Instead, it's largely frozen in polar ice caps or subsurface soil, with some atmospheric vapor. Recent discoveries by NASA's Mars Reconnaissance Orbiter (MRO) also hint at the existence of liquid water during warmer seasons, albeit in very salty, briny form.

Initial Mars colonists would likely target these ice stores first to obtain water. The process would require mining the ice and treating it in purification systems. However, this process is energy-intensive and challenging, given Mars' frigid average temperatures of -80 degrees F (-62 degrees C). Developing viable and efficient ice-water extraction techniques is an ongoing research pursuit in NASA and other space agencies.

6.2. Breathing Space: Creating a Martian Atmosphere

Mars' atmosphere, composed mainly of carbon dioxide (95%), is not breathable for humans. Moreover, the thin Martian atmosphere fails to provide adequate shielding from the sun's ultraviolet radiation. Therefore, creating a habitable atmosphere is a vital cog in the Martian survival mechanism.

The first approach to producing oxygen may rely on a process known as electrolysis, specifically splitting water molecules into hydrogen and oxygen. The Mars Oxygen ISRU Experiment (MOXIE) on the Mars 2020 Perseverance rover is a precursor for such technology. It seeks to produce oxygen directly from the Martian atmosphere—a more sustainable long-term solution—but this technology is still in its nascent stages.

Protecting humans from cosmic-rays and solar radiation requires generating an artificial magnetosphere or building habitats with radiation shielding. Institutions such as NASA and SpaceX propose deploying large inflatable domes or developing underground Martian bases for this purpose.

6.3. Shelter: Homes away from Home

Providing prospective Mars inhabitants with safe, robust shelter involves overcoming the planet's environmental adversities, such as rarefied atmospheric conditions, the presence of dust storms, and the high radiation levels.

Recently, there have been proposals for constructing habitats using Martian regolith (soil) as it is rich in iron oxides, which can be formed into a concrete-like material. NASA's 3D-Printed Habitat

Challenge has spurred research into creating such livable spaces to counter the logistical challenge of carrying pre-built modules from Earth.

Another approach involves constructing habitats underground, where natural shielding is offered against harmful radiation. Lava tubes, caves formed by lava flows, are possible locations for these subterranean homes, although they present additional challenges in terms of light and power.

6.4. Food: Sustaining Life on Mars

Food production represents another grand challenge on Mars—a planet whose soil contains toxic material unfit for planting crops. While delivering supplies from Earth is plausible for initial expeditions, it becomes impractical for sustained stay or larger colonies.

Hydroponics, or growing plants without soil, utilizing nutrient solutions, is a promising solution. The Mars Desert Research Station (MDRS) is conducting experimental research on this front, attempting to grow a variety of plants, including lettuces, radishes, and herbs.

Additionally, there's ongoing research targeting the removal or alteration of the toxic Martian regolith for agriculture purposes. NASA's Mars rover, Perseverance, will further investigate Mars' soil composition and potential toxicity mitigation methods.

6.5. Energy: Powering the Red Planet

Establishing a reliable, efficient power source on Mars is integral to all facets of survival, including water extraction, refuge heating, oxygen production, and food cultivation. Mars's distance from the sun (about 50% farther than Earth) makes solar power generation less efficient than on Earth.

Solar power is the most likely initial source of energy due to its relative simplicity and successful use in missions such as the Mars Exploration Rovers and the Mars Science Laboratory. However, dust storms pose a challenge as they can significantly reduce power production by blocking sunlight.

To provide consistent power for a Mars base, future technologies could harness nuclear energy. NASA's Kilopower project is developing small-scale, highly efficient nuclear power systems for space deployment. Wind power is another considered alternative given Mars' frequent high-speed winds.

Survival on Mars is an intricate network of multifaceted challenges, each providing both a hurdle and an opportunity for human ingenuity. With every problem we solve on the way to making Mars habitable, we learn more about living sustainably not only on another planet but also here on Earth. As this chapter reveals, there are no easy solutions—but by acknowledging and facing these obstacles, we take another step toward our cosmic future. The following chapters will delve into the sociopolitical and ethical considerations of Mars colonization, providing the full picture of the intricate leap that awaits humanity.

Chapter 7. Bioengineering: Terraforming Mars

Terraforming Mars is no small endeavour; it requires a vast amount of knowledge across a variety of scientific and engineering fields. Let's delve into the concept, the processes, and the technologies that can make this magnificent quest achievable.

Starting with the vision of creating a 'second Earth,' scientists have spent decades examining our neighboring planet's makeup and exploring terraforming possibilities. The fulfillment of this vision paves the way to becoming an interplanetary species, safeguarding against potential extinction events, or accommodate a growing population split between two planets.

7.1. Understanding Mars' Current State

Before delving into the mechanics of terraforming, it's beneficial to understand the current Martian landscape, which, despite shared characteristics with Earth, poses significant challenges. Mars is cold, with temperatures around -80 degrees Fahrenheit on average, and has a horrifically thin atmosphere, composed mostly of carbon dioxide, with hardly any breathable oxygen. Its soil or "regolith" is toxic, with a high perchlorate content, and it lacks a magnetic field to shield against dangerous cosmic rays.

The terraforming process, therefore, must address all these challenges - it needs to warm the planet, increase the atmospheric pressure, introduce breathable air, detoxify the soil, and establish radiation protection.

7.2. Warming the Red Planet

Initiating a global warming process, similar to the one inadvertently set in motion on Earth, stands as the initial step towards making Mars habitable. By deliberately increasing the planet's heat trapped in the atmosphere — through a greenhouse effect — Mars' temperature can raise enough to allow water to be stable in liquid form.

There are several methods scientists consider for triggering this Martian warming. One is through the emission of greenhouse gasses. Importantly, Mars' polar ice caps contain carbon dioxide (CO_2), a potent greenhouse gas. By sublimating these ice caps using large mirrors in space or dark soot to increase their absorption of sunlight could release the trapped CO_2.

Another method is the production and introduction of super greenhouse gasses, such as perfluorocarbons (PFCs). PFCs are significantly more potent than CO_2 and can be produced sustainably.

7.3. Building up the Martian Atmosphere

Atmospheric pressure on Mars is very low — less than 1% of Earth's. Therefore, after increasing the planet's temperature, the next priority would be to build up its atmosphere. This would not only provide the pressure required for humans to survive without a spacesuit but also create conditions suitable for liquid water on the planet's surface.

The released CO_2 from the polar ice caps would give an appreciable start, but additional measures would be needed. Producing gasses like nitrogen and argon that form the bulk of Earth's atmosphere could be achieved through in situ resource utilization (ISRU), processing the Martian regolith and atmosphere. ISRU would be a crucial part of any long-term human presence on Mars.

7.4. Creating a Breathable Atmosphere

Once the atmospheric pressure is at a breathable level, the introduction of oxygen would be the next step. Oxygen makes up around 21% of Earth's atmosphere, and a similar concentration would be ideal on Mars.

There are multiple proposed methods for generating oxygen on Mars. One is through electrolysis, which involves passing an electric current through water (H_2O) to separate it into hydrogen (H_2) and oxygen (O_2). Another method is through MOXIE (Mars Oxygen In-Situ Resource Utilization Experiment), a technology already being tested on NASA's Perseverance rover to convert Martian atmospheric CO_2 into oxygen.

7.5. Detoxifying the Martian Regolith

The Martian soil, rich in toxic perchlorates, is a significant obstacle that needs to be addressed for human survival and agriculture. There are several potential ways to detoxify it. One would be through the introduction of genetically engineered microorganisms that can break down these compounds or the use of chemicals to leach out the toxins.

7.6. Providing Radiation Protection

One of the most challenging aspects of terraforming Mars is dealing with the high levels of radiation. Without a magnetic shield like Earth's, the surface of Mars is lethally irradiated.

Engineering solutions such as building habitats with radiation shields or genetically modifying humans to be more radiation-resistant are possible, but these are the areas where the most innovation will be required.

Chapter 8. Going Beyond Terraforming Mars

Terraforming Mars is a striking example of bioengineering's ultimate potential. It's an audacious project that might take hundreds if not thousands of years to come to fruition. But as we find ourselves standing on the threshold of becoming a space-faring civilization, we're more than ever aware of our responsibility not just to explore, but to protect and cherish all life within our reach.

The realization of this multi-century project necessitates the concerted effort of scientists, engineers, and decision-makers worldwide. It needs continuous technological innovation, emerging advancements in bioengineering, political will, and above all, a shared vision for our future as a multiplanetary species. Mars is not just our neighbor; it's our next colossal challenge, and possibly, our second home.

Chapter 9. Potential Creators of a New Civilization: Who are the Stakeholders?

The successful colonization of Mars, our neighboring celestial body, represents a vast collaboration of visionaries, experts, and enthusiasts across the globe, each bringing to the table unique skills, knowledge, and perspective. This vast pool of involved parties, from government entities to private entities, from scientists to potential colonial inhabitants, collectively make up the mighty force behind the actualization of this once unfathomable dream. This chapter offers an in-depth examination of these key players, painting a vivid picture of their roles, objectives, challenges, and anticipation in this grand endeavor.

9.1. The Guardians of the Sky: Space Agencies

The prominent space agencies worldwide, notably NASA (USA), ESA (European Space Agency), Roscosmos (Russia), ISRO (Indian Space Research Organisation), and CNSA (China National Space Administration), act as the designated guardians and pioneers of humanity's extraterrestrial pursuits. Long before the considerable interest from the private sector, these agencies ignited the path to Mars through numerous missions, each enhancing our understanding of the Red Planet.

However, their purpose extends beyond research. With decades of experience, their expertise and stringent protocols set the benchmark for space exploration. They regulate the international utilization of space for peaceful means while ensuring the minimization of cosmic debris—remnants of human activity in space.

The race to Mars, however, tests their essence. As convergence grows between these international agencies and the private sector's might, a new model of cooperative public-private partnership is inevitable. This converged vision paves the path for laws, policies, and plans directing Mars colonization.

9.2. Entrepreneurs with Starry Eyes: Private Space Companies

Multitudes of private entities harness the vast potential of space exploration today, spearheaded by the likes of SpaceX, Blue Origin, and Virgin Galactic, among others. These companies, capitalized by visionary entrepreneurs such as Elon Musk and Jeff Bezos, outlook a future where Mars is not merely an exploratory destination but a practical, inhabitant colony.

SpaceX's Starship, for instance, is being developed with the ambitious vision of transporting as many as 100 individuals to Mars per trip. Likewise, Blue Origin plans to foster millions of people living and working in space.

These companies present an agile, innovative, and extremely well-funded approach that boldly pushes the boundaries of what's possible, making space more accessible. Despite being fraught with uncertainty and challenges, their tenacity propels us closer to the dream – colonization of Mars.

9.3. The Crucibles of Knowledge: Space Research Institutions

From mapping the Martian terrain to understanding its weather patterns and potential for sustaining life, research institutions dedicated to space exploration provide indispensable knowledge.

This includes institutions such as Massachusetts Institute of Technology (MIT), California Institute of Technology (Caltech), and Stanford, among others, working on breakthrough scientific and technological research. Their work ranges from elaborating on propulsion techniques to developing sustainable life-support systems critical for human survival on Mars.

9.4. The Torchbearers: Potential Mars Colonists

Potential Martian colonists and their willingness to embark on a possibly perilous journey represent the human spirit's audacity. As early settlers, their role, though fraught with dangers, holds the promise of profound implications for future generations. Their resilience, adaptability, and ingenuity will ultimately determine the success or failure of this remarkable endeavor.

Settlers will likely span a wide array of professionals, including engineers, doctors, scientists, and architects, who can maintain and enhance the colony over time. Additionally, given the physical and psychological challenges facing Mars' citizens, considerable conditioning is required to adapt to their new home.

9.5. The Custodians of Order: Policymakers and Governments

The successful colonization of Mars also brings the question of governance and jurisprudence to the forefront. Deciding the legal ownership of land, resource management, conflict resolution, and ensuring peace between Earth and Mars introduces unprecedented complexities. Therefore, the role of policymakers and governments is and remains fundamentally crucial. The challenge lies in formulating and executing laws that are just and sustainable, regulating human activities while protecting the precarious Martian ecosystem.

9.6. The Sentinels of Morality: Ethicists and Environmentalists

Ethicists argue the moral assumption, rights and wrongs of colonizing Mars, while environmentalists monitor the potential ecological impact on the alien ecosystem. Together, they serve as our morality compass, ensuring that our actions do not lead to catastrophic, irreversible consequences.

In conclusion, every stakeholder, with their distinctive roles and capabilities, holds a piece of the colossal puzzle of Martian colonization. Their collaborative efforts draw humanity substantially closer to the ambitious reality of establishing a thriving Martian civilization. This ambitious aim wouldn't merely redefine humanity's cosmic destiny but also recalibrate our understanding of life itself. Undeterbly, the stakes are high and the challenges are formidable - but so too is the collective spirit of mankind.

Chapter 10. Sociopolitical Implications of Mars Colonization

Space colonization transcends beyond the constraints of technology and science, raising a myriad of sociopolitical implications demanding thoughtful consideration. These manifest in aspects like establishing governance, societal and cultural development, economic and resource-related implications, international cooperation, and issues of space law. This chapter aims at diving deep into these spheres, peeling back the layers of these intricate aspects.

10.1. Governance and Legal Framework on Mars

In the advent of Martian colonization, one of the first challenges would involve formulating a unique governance and legal structure suitable to the needs and constraints of the Martian environment. So far, international law, like the Outer Space Treaty (1967), prevents any country from exercising sovereignty over celestial bodies. Consequently, no singular nation, private entity, or individual can lay claim on Mars or any part thereof.

A new paradigm of laws needs to be implemented, considering human rights, duties, and liabilities of colonists. These laws need to tread a fine line, ensuring they are not too restrictive to throttle innovation and advancement and not too lenient to cause chaos and lawlessness.

10.2. Ensuring Societal and Cultural Evolution

Building a sustainable society on Mars would require careful planning and management, accounting for population diversity, cultural traditions, and social stability. Colonies on Mars need to be mindful not to replicate the societal ills of earth such as discrimination, inequality, and social unrest.

Cultural evolution is another significant consideration. Striking a balance between preserving earthly traditions and fostering an authentic Martian culture would be a monumental task. The new society would need to be flexible enough to accommodate cultural transformation and adaptation, yet resilient enough to endure cultural shocks and destabilization.

10.3. Economic Considerations and Resource Management

Considering the economics of colonization, Mars would need to be self-sufficient to avoid dependence on Earth for resources. Initiatives such as In-Situ Resource Utilization (ISRU) strategies need to be employed for the production of water, food, and energy. Furthermore, the economic feasibility of Martian colonization is also dependent on the initiation of martian industries and the potential for Mars-Earth trade.

Effective management of Martian resources would be another key challenge. There would be a dire need to develop efficient systems to manage scarcity and distribution, while also ensuring the sustainability and minimal impact on the Martian environment.

10.4. International Cooperation and Security

Colonization of Mars necessitates international cooperation. Collaborative projects offer opportunities to pool resources, share risks, and enhance scientific outcomes. However, they also open avenues for political tensions, territorial disputes, and conflicts.

Another aspect is the security associated with colonization. Ensuring the security of the colonists from external threats, managing disputes between colonists, and the establishment of enforcement agencies will require careful strategization and consensus.

10.5. Revisiting Space Law

Mars colonization will require redefining current space laws. Legal decisions regarding property rights, mineral rights, environmental obligations, and the potential for militarization and weaponization of Mars will be put into focus.

Establishing these laws would require international negotiation and agreement. However, consensus on these issues, given the different national interests, may be a formidable challenge.

In conclusion, Mars colonization extends far beyond the technicalities of rocket science and engineering. It calls for well-drawn strategies to cater to sociopolitical, cultural, economic, and legal aspects that accompany the colonization of a new planet. It can be a groundbreaking endeavor, given that it's maneuvered wisely, creating a more diversified, resilient, and sustainable interplanetary species.

Chapter 11. Future Cautions: Risks and Remedies

Exploring the frontiers of space has always been a high-risk, high-reward venture for humankind. Mars, with its inclement climatic conditions and logistical unknowns, is no exception. Despite consuming centuries of our collective imagination, the actuality of colonizing Mars poses substantial challenges that need to be addressed meticulously.

11.1. Technological Risks and Remedies

One of the most pressing risks revolves around technological limitations. Current technologies are inadequate for a sustainable Martian colony considering factors such as fuel, oxygen, food, and recycling waste.

The remedy lies in persistent research and development. Many space agencies and private organizations are leveraging technological advancements, such as artificial intelligence and robotics, to devise solutions to these challenges. Additionally, the rapid development of in-situ resource utilization (ISRU) technologies, capable of mining and refining materials on site, are promising.

11.2. Radiation Exposure and Countermeasures

A more imminent threat to Martian settlers would be radiation. Mars has a depleted magnetosphere, unlike Earth, leading to high exposure levels that could potentially cause cancer and other diseases.

The most practical solution would be to live underground, where Martian soil could act as a natural protective barrier. Also, advancements in radiation shielding materials and suits could aid in mitigating this risk.

11.3. Gravity Conundrums and Solutions

Another challenge, often underappreciated, is the Martian gravity, which is roughly one-third that of Earth. Over time, low gravity can cause muscle atrophy and bone density loss.

To counteract this, Colony habitats may need to have sections where artificial gravity is created, possibly by means of rotation. Moreover, specially designed physical conditioning regimens would be crucial for colonists.

11.4. Psychological Risks and Resilience Strategies

The mental health of colonists is another concern. Isolation, a harsh environment, and the immense distance from Earth could induce stress, depression, or other psychological issues.

Several measures can be taken here. Fostering a close-knit and supportive community, virtual connectivity with family and friends back on Earth, and psychological aid in the form of therapy should be integral to the project.

11.5. Sociopolitical Hurdles and Pathways

The colonization of Mars would not just be a technical endeavor, but also a sociopolitical one. There would likely be disputes over territory and resources, and a lack of consensus on governance models.

International cooperation and legally binding treaties could be the answer here. Creating a mutually agreed upon framework for Martian colonization could prevent turf wars and ensure that Mars does not become a stage for Earthly disputes.

11.6. Interplanetary Contamination and Prevention

The prospect of Mars colonization raises the issue of interplanetary contamination. Both 'Forward contamination' (from Earth to Mars) and 'Backward contamination' (from Mars to Earth) are serious concerns.

Strategies for preventing contamination include sterilizing equipment before launch, using controlled environments for handling Martian samples on Earth, and minimizing the use of resources that could potentially harbor Earth microbes.

Despite the herculean obstacles in store, the eventual fruits of successful Martian Colonization - human survival, scientific progress, and the enchanting spectacle of humanity becoming a multiplanetary species - are indeed tantalizing. Solutions to these prospective issues lie in collaboration, innovation, and persistence. In time, we may indeed see Martian sunsets become as routine as those on Earth.

Chapter 12. Towards a New Dawn: The Future of Mars Colonization

It is the dawn of an era unlike any other in human history. We, as a species, have always looked towards the heavens, our curiosity piqued by the infinite worlds beyond our own. Of all celestial bodies within our reach, none have captivated us quite like Mars. Its flaming red glimmer in the night sky personifies humanity's greatest challenge yet - colonizing a planet other than Earth.

12.1. A Streak for the Stars

The 21st-century space race is much different from the 1960s competition between the United States and the Soviet Union for dominance over lunar exploration. Today, it's not just national entities with space ambitions. Private companies, spearheaded by revolutionary minds like Elon Musk and Jeff Bezos, have thrown their hats in the ring with the goal of landing humans on Mars and creating a sustainable presence there.

SpaceX's Starship, currently in development, is designed to carry up to 100 passengers to the Red Planet, with plans for the first manned mission tentatively scheduled for the mid-2020s. Simultaneously, NASA's Artemis program, with the goal of returning humans to the Moon, serves as a stepping stone towards a much more ambitious objective - Mars.

However, reaching Mars is only the first chapter in this epic adventure. The real task is making our stay there sustainable.

12.2. Turning the Tides

Mars is incredibly hostile to human life. It has a thin atmosphere, which is mostly carbon dioxide and does little to protect the surface from harmful radiation. It's cold, with an average temperature of -80 degrees Fahrenheit, and the planet has almost no water that's readily accessible.

During the past few decades, Mars rovers such as Spirit, Opportunity, and more recently, Perseverance, have been gathering data on the planet's geography, climate, and potential for life. They've sent back promising information that hints at the existence of underground water and a past history that's more conducive to life.

Creating a suitable living environment involves altering the Martian climate - an ambitious endeavor known as terraforming. This could involve redirecting comets and asteroids rich in water and carbon dioxide to Mars to thicken its atmosphere, or using nuclear weapons to sublimate its polar ice caps. However, these ideas are currently purely theoretic and would require technology well beyond our current capabilities.

12.3. Forestalling the Fallout

While establishing a sustainable human presence on the Red Planet might seem like pure science fiction, the less glamorous realities of interplanetary colonization hide in the details. Cosmic radiation, lonesomeness, and boredom pose as psychological breakers breaching colonizers' sanity walls. The inherent danger of living on a non-Earth body, coupled with the long communication delays with home, could induce isolation and stress in the inhabitants.

Going forward, special emphasis must be placed on mental health as an integral part of mission planning. This includes stringent mental health screening for candidates, a robust support system that includes ample leisure activities and regular communication with families and psychiatrists on Earth, and a contingent response protocol in case of a psychological crisis.

12.4. A Martian Magna Carta

Aside from the physical and psychological challenges of Martian colonization, there are critical legal and societal implications as well. Who will own Mars? Will it be the property of whoever gets there first, or is it a scientific commons, as decided by the Outer Space Treaty of 1967? What laws will govern its inhabitants?

These intricacies need thorough deliberation. As we're venturing into uncharted waters, a sustainable society on Mars would require the establishment of a governance body. Whether this will take the form of an entirely new "Martian" legal framework, or an extension of the existing international law, remains to be seen.

12.5. In Search of Martian Gold

The Financial burden of Mars colonization raises many questions about its feasibility. The cost of building, launching, and supporting spaceships; developing and maintaining Martian infrastructure; and ensuring regular supply missions could run into the trillions.

Public-private partnerships like SpaceX and NASA can share the financial burden. However, colonization would need to make economic sense as well. A self-sustaining Mars colony would require a stable economy, profit-bearing industries, and a circulation of Martian currency.

Potential revenue streams could include space tourism, scientific research, media rights, and exploiting Mars' resources. The discovery of valuable minerals or other resources on Mars could help offset the cost of colonization.

12.6. Homeward Bound

The eventual aim of Mars colonization is not to make a one-way trip, but to facilitate regular travel between Earth and Mars. Then, Mars would not just be a refuge for humanity in the event of a catastrophic occurrence on Earth, but a step towards becoming an interplanetary species.

For this to happen, large-scale production of fuel on Mars is a necessity. The vital component is creating a propellant plant, which Elon Musk, for instance, envisions manufacturing methane and oxygen from Martian carbon dioxide and subsurface water ice.

12.7. The Red Frontier

In essence, Mars colonization is more than just an engineering problem. It's a strategic endeavor that demands international cooperation, innovative business models, political will, a revolutionary legal framework, and attention to human health and well-being. It is an exploratory journey in the truest sense - towards understanding our potential as a species and our place in the cosmic ocean.

Though the Red Planet presents abundant challenges, it also teases with immense opportunities. The path to a permanent human presence on Mars is complex and ridden with uncertainty. Yet, as we stand on the cusp of this novel dawn, humans persist in the relentless pursuit of knowledge and exploration, undeterred by the demanding path that illuminates the way to our next celestial home. Mars.

www.ingramcontent.com/pod-product-compliance
Lightning Source LLC
LaVergne TN
LVHW051630050326
832903LV00033B/4714